Student Booster:
Writing Description

By
CINDY BARDEN

COPYRIGHT © 2003 Mark Twain Media, Inc.

ISBN 1-58037-245-7

Printing No. CD-1591

Mark Twain Media, Inc., Publishers
Distributed by Carson-Dellosa Publishing Company, Inc.

Table of Contents

Introduction to the Teacher

Writing Description provides students with an outlet to express thoughts and feelings, to explore ideas, to entertain, and to have fun.

This book encourages students to write descriptions of people, places, things, and abstract ideas using adjectives and lively verbs. Students will create a Venn diagram to compare and contrast people; explore idioms, similes, and metaphors; and test their powers of observation. Activities also include *Adjective Charades*, finishing a drawing based on a description, and writing paragraphs describing sensory experiences.

Descriptive Writing

Be Specific

Descriptive writing provides vivid details. The key to a good description is to be as specific as possible.

The main purpose of a description is to enable the reader to picture what you're describing. These tips will help you to write better descriptions.

 Decide on a topic: Before you begin writing, decide on a topic. If your topic is too broad, you may not be able to cover it completely. If your topic is too narrow, you may not have enough to write about.

 Gather ideas: This can include jotting down ideas, checking reference sources, doing surveys, gathering data, etc.

 Organize your material: Describing events in order works best for many topics. It provides a time sense of what happened first, next, and last. You can also outline your topic and organize the main ideas in order of importance, with examples or explanations for each main point.

 Add details, descriptions, and examples: Details related to the main topic provide the reader with a clear image.

 Edit and revise: When you finish your first draft, ask yourself:

- Is my writing clear and concise?
- Is any important information missing?
- Is there too much or too little detail?
- Did I use complete sentences?
- Did I stick to my topic?
- Did I include an interesting topic sentence and conclusion?

 Proofread: Correct errors in grammar, punctuation, and spelling.

Double-check: Go back and read through your final copy one more time.

Name: _____   Date: _____

A Delicious Paragraph

A **paragraph** is a group of sentences about a specific topic. An interesting paragraph is like a tasty sandwich.

When you bite into a sandwich, the top piece of bread is the first thing you taste. The **topic sentence** of a paragraph is like the top piece of bread. It introduces the main idea of a paragraph. If the topic sentence is not fresh and interesting, the reader won't want to bite any further.

Interesting topic sentences encourage readers to bite further into the paragraph.

Write two different topic sentences for each subject.

1. a trip in a canoe _____

    _____

    _____

    _____

2. being lost in a forest _____

    _____

    _____

    _____

3. taking care of a pet _____

    _____

    _____

    _____

4. a person you admire _____

    _____

    _____

    _____

5. Save this page to use with the next activity.

Name: _____ Date: _____

Sliced Bananas and Peanut Butter With Liver Sausage and Pickles on Rye

A great slice of bread alone does not make a memorable sandwich. The middle of the sandwich needs to include interesting and tasty ingredients.

Topic sentences are followed by **supporting sentences** that provide interesting information, give examples, or provide additional details and descriptions.

1. Write two sentences that could follow each topic sentence.

   As soon as I woke up, I knew it was going to be one of those days when nothing goes right.

   _____

   _____

   _____

   _____

   As darkness crept toward us, we huddled closer to the fire, listening to the sounds of the waking forest.

   _____

   _____

   _____

   _____

2. Rewrite your best topic sentence from the last activity. Add supporting sentences.

   _____

   _____

   _____

   _____

   _____

   _____

   _____

   _____

3. Save this page to use with the next activity.

Name: _____ Date: _____

Good to the Last Bite

The bottom piece of bread in a sandwich is like the **conclusion sentence** in a paragraph. Without the second piece of bread, the sandwich would fall apart. The conclusion sentence restates the main idea or sums up the main points in a paragraph.

1. Write a conclusion sentence for one of the three topics on the last page.

   _____

   _____

2. Cut out a picture from an old magazine that shows any type of scenery, preferably one without people. The scene could be of a city, mountain, rain forest, or even under the ocean. Imagine visiting this place.

3. Write a topic sentence you could use to begin a paragraph describing your visit to the place shown in the picture.

   _____

   _____

4. List details you might see, hear, feel, taste, and touch if you were there in person.

   _____

   _____

   _____

5. Write a conclusion sentence to sum up a paragraph about your visit to this place.

   _____

   _____

   _____

6. On your own paper, write a descriptive paragraph about any person, place, thing, or event. You can use any of the topics or sentences you wrote about in the last two activities.

7. Reread what you wrote. Keep these questions in mind as you revise your descriptive paragraph.

   • Can you make the topic sentence more interesting?
   • Did you include descriptions, details, and/or examples in the middle of the paragraph?
   • Did your conclusion sum up the main idea of the paragraph?

Name: _____ Date: _____

A Purple Alien Wearing Green- and Yellow-Striped Pajamas

Adjectives are words that describe nouns or other adjectives. *Red, frizzy, enormous,* and *lazy* are adjectives. Adjectives help the reader to form a mental picture of a person, place, or thing.

Underline the adjectives.

1. a large shaggy dog with floppy ears

2. a tiny gray mouse with a long thin tail

3. a freckled boy with red hair wearing a green baseball cap

4. an old chair with a broken leg, sagging springs, and moth holes

Write adjectives to describe each noun.

5. alien _____

6. tiger _____

7. sky _____

8. whale _____

9. flower _____

10. shoes _____

Fill in the blanks with adjectives to complete the sentences.

11. The _____, _____ woman with the
    _____, _____ hat raced quickly through the
    _____, _____ alley.

12. As the _____ boy wandered farther into the _____
    woods, the _____ roots of the trees and their
    _____ limbs seemed to be trying to trap him.

13. When the _____, _____ sun rose above the
    _____ hill, it looked like a _____ ball of fire.

14. Maria found a _____, _____ bag in the
    _____ parking lot behind the _____ factory.

15. Petting the _____, _____ snake was the last thing
    Jeremiah wanted to do.

Name: _____ Date: _____

When you write, you become the eyes of the reader. Descriptive writing uses adjectives to provide the reader with a clear picture of people, places, things, and ideas.

Sight words include descriptions of color, shape, size, and texture.

Each of these phrases describes a type of container. Read the description, then draw the container. Use colored pencils or pens.

1. a rotten, wooden chest with rusted hinges

2. a green and red plastic toy box

3. a large, shiny, metal safe

4. a square, battered cardboard box

5. an empty, rectangular glass aquarium

6. a triangular stone pyramid

7. Decide on an object to describe. On your own paper, write a paragraph describing that object in detail, but do not name the object. Call it "Object X" if you need to use a word. Describe the size, shape, color, texture, and other features of the object.

8. When you finish your paragraph, trade papers with a partner. Read each other's descriptions. See if you can guess the object being described.

Name: _____ Date: _____

Hear It!

Sounds are everywhere. What do you hear when you close your eyes and listen? Can you hear the motor on your refrigerator? The hum of your computer? Traffic noises? Children playing? Birds singing?

Buzz, creak, howl, roar, cheer, rumble, crash, and *squeak* describe sounds. **Onomatopoeia** uses words that imitate a sound. The words can be real, like *crunch,* or made-up, like *ka-pow* and *ka-boom.*

Write words to describe these sounds. You can use real words, or make up your own.

1. Walking barefoot through squishy mud _____

_____

_____

2. A rocky shore with huge waves crashing _____

_____

_____

3. Going down a huge waterslide _____

_____

_____

4. What you hear right now if you close your eyes and listen _____

_____

_____

5. On your own paper, describe an experience so that the reader can hear the sounds of the event. (Experiences could be attending the circus, playing football, watching a parade, walking down a busy city street, or sitting at an airport.)

6. When you finish, proofread, edit, revise, and rewrite your description.

Name: _____ Date: _____

Smell It!

Imagine watching a movie that provided not only sound and pictures, but also smells! Describing smells in writing adds to the reader's sense of being part of the scene.

Write words to describe these smells:

1. a damp fall day after a heavy rain _____

    _____

2. a soap factory _____

    _____

3. a candy store _____

    _____

4. a freshly mowed lawn _____

    _____

5. a locker room after a basketball game _____

    _____

6. your favorite perfume or aftershave _____

    _____

7. a loaf of homemade bread _____

    _____

8. a hospital or medical clinic _____

    _____

9. On your own paper, describe a place that has many smells, like a restaurant, bakery, kitchen, or garden. Use sensory words that describe the various aromas.

10. When you finish, proofread, edit, revise, and rewrite your description.

Did You Know? Movies with "Smell-O-Vision" were first introduced in 1960, but they never became popular.

Name: _____ Date: _____

Taste It!

Imagine eating a bowl of cold, creamy, mint chocolate ice cream on a hot summer day. *Cold, creamy, mint,* and *chocolate* describe the taste, temperature, and texture of the ice cream. *Sweet, hot, sour, crunchy, tangy, salty,* and *bitter* are other adjectives that describe taste and texture.

1. Write taste, temperature, and texture words to describe each item.

    A. stale bread _____

    _____

    B. a cup of hot cocoa with marshmallows _____

    _____

    C. a steaming bowl of spicy chili _____

    _____

    D. a two-day-old deluxe pizza with 10 toppings _____

    _____

    E. mashed potatoes and gravy _____

    _____

2. List six fruit flavors. _____

    _____

3. List six vegetable flavors. _____

    _____

4. List six words that describe the texture of food.

    _____

    _____

5. On your own paper, describe your favorite meal so that the reader will be able to "taste" all the goodies.

6. When you finish, proofread, edit, revise, and rewrite your description.

Name: _____ Date: _____

Touch It!

We use our hands to feel the texture of objects. Sandpaper feels rough and gritty. *Bumpy, smooth, wet, warm,* and *soft* are other words that describe how something feels.

Your sense of touch is not limited to your hands. Cold rain on your face, the wind blowing through your hair, the hot sun beating on your skin, and walking barefoot through thick, cool, squishy mud are also sensory experiences.

List words to describe these experiences.

1. cuddling with a fuzzy blanket _____

   _____

2. walking on a cold, windy, rainy day_____

   _____

3. lifting a heavy wooden box _____

   _____

4. running a long race _____

   _____

5. jumping into cold water _____

   _____

Most experiences involve using several senses at the same time.

6. Which senses would you use if you were a drummer in a marching band?

   _____

   _____

7. Which senses would you use if you were chopping onions?

   _____

   _____

8. On your own paper, describe a personal experience so the reader can share the feel and texture of the event. (Experiences could be falling asleep in a hammock, wading in a creek, or standing on a hill on a windy day.)

9. When you finish, proofread, edit, revise, and rewrite your description.

Name: _____ Date: _____

Sensory Words

Work with a partner or small group. Fill in words for each sense that begin with each letter of the alphabet. Use any part of speech.

	Sight	Hearing	Smell	Taste	Touch
a			aroma		
b					
c					
d					
e					
f					
g	green				
h					
i					
j				juicy	
k					
l					
m					
n					
o					
p					
q					
r					
s					
t					
u					
v					velvety
w		whisper			
x					
y					
z					

Name: _____ Date: _____

Show Me in Words

1. On your own paper, write a paragraph to describe one of these scenes. Use sensory words to paint a picture of the sights, sounds, smells, tastes, and feel of the scene.

   At the circus: A visit to a circus involves the use of all of your senses as you watch the clowns, hear the elephants, smell the popcorn, taste the cotton candy, and feel its stickiness on your face.

   Visit a deli: Describe a visit to a busy neighborhood deli around noon when people are ordering lunch and drinks. What do you see, hear, smell, taste, and touch?

   At the beach: Describe the sights, sounds, smells, tastes, and feel of a trip to a crowded beach on a day when the temperature is close to 100 degrees Fahrenheit.

   In your neighborhood: Imagine taking your orange juice and toast outside early in the morning after a rainy night. Use sensory words to describe what you see, hear, taste, smell, and feel as you sit on the front steps.

   Brrr!: Although the sun is shining, the temperature is only around 20 degrees Fahrenheit. Describe what it would be like to build a snowman or go sledding, skating, or skiing on a bright winter day.

   Clues to the Chocolate Chip Cookie Caper:
   Imagine being the first police officer at the scene of a robbery in a bakery. Someone stole all of the chocolate chip cookies! Use sensory words to describe what you see, hear, taste, smell, and feel as you investigate the crime and look for clues.

2. When you finish your first draft, edit, revise, and proofread your paragraph. Draw a picture to go with your paragraph, or use computer clip art to create a scene.

Name: _____ Date: _____

Pretty Flowers + Pretty Garden = Pretty Dull

Most people wouldn't want to eat the same foods at every meal. That would be very dull! They wouldn't want to watch the same movie or read the same book over and over, either. People enjoy variety.

Variety makes your writing more interesting. **Synonyms** are words that mean the same, or nearly the same, thing. You can find synonyms for many words in a **thesaurus**.

Write two or more synonyms for each word. Use a thesaurus if you need ideas.

Sensational   TERRIFIC   Marvelous   Magnificent   Wonderful   Superb   Spectacular

1. run _____

2. saw _____

3. heard _____

4. funny _____

5. strange _____

6. nice _____

7. tame _____

8. loud _____

9. exciting _____

In the following paragraph, the word *pretty* is used five times. Dull and boring! Rewrite the paragraph, and replace the word *pretty* with five different words. Change any other words that you think are dull.

10. Rachel wandered happily through the pretty garden. She had never seen so many pretty flowers in her life. Some were so pretty that they looked like rainbows. The pretty flowers in the pretty garden had as many colors as a box of 64 crayons.

_____

_____

_____

_____

Teacher/Parent Page: Preparation for Adjective Charades

See instructions on page 15.

chilly	round	magical	graceful
pretty	large	small	high
handsome	fierce	sad	tall
happy	smelly	pleasant	red
soft	broken	scared	loud
low	dark	green	sharp
dry	cute	black	elegant
light	blue	soft	great
silky	frightened	handy	icy
empty	jolly	kind	lovely
dull	merry	pink	quiet
silly	talented	excellent	glad
lucky	honest	reliable	quick
lonely	friendly	spotted	fast
wooden	full	metallic	deep

Teacher/Parent Page

Directions for "Adjective Charades"

To play Adjective Charades, make a copy of the adjective list on page 14, cut the words apart, and place the slips of paper in a bag or box. Let students take turns drawing a slip of paper and acting out the adjective through pantomime. The student who guesses the word correctly takes the next turn.

Extension Activity: Adjective Hunt

Give students time to look around and list ten objects they can see in the room. Next to each noun, have them write three or more adjectives to describe that object.

Students can take turns naming adjectives they wrote for any one noun, without naming the object. Have the other students guess what object in the room the adjectives describe.

Preparation for "Are You Observant?" Activity

<u>Before</u> students complete the activity on the next page, plan to take them someplace they've never been before: a friend's house, the teachers' lounge, the principal's office, the school kitchen, a store at a mall, a restaurant, or any place that isn't too large.

Make notes about the room in advance by filling in the blanks on the next page, but don't give students a copy of the page until after they return to the classroom.

When they arrive, tell students they will be testing their powers of observation. They should look closely at the room. Ask them to concentrate on really seeing the room, the furnishings, the walls, the ceiling, and the floor. Give them about 5 to 10 minutes to look around.

After you return to the classroom, ask them to complete the "Are You Observant?" Activity with as many details as they can remember.

When they finish, talk about the different features of the room and their answers. How many details did most people miss? What does that tell them about how observant they are?

Name: _____ Date: _____

"Are You Observant?" Activity

Answer the following questions on your own paper. Fill in as much as you remember about the room you observed.

- What shape was the room?

- About how large was it?

- How high was the ceiling?

- What color was it?

- Describe the color and type of floor (carpet, wood, tile, etc.).

- Describe the color and type of walls (paneling, painted, wallpaper, etc.).

- Describe the decorations on the walls.

- Were there any plants in the room? If so, about how many, and what type?

- Describe the furniture: size, shape, color, and any other details you can remember.

- Describe any knickknacks or statues in the room.

- What could you smell in the room?

- What sounds could you hear in the room?

- How many doors were in the room? How many windows?

- Describe the curtains or blinds.

- Is there anything else memorable about the room?

Name: _____ Date: _____

Finish the Pictures

"His eyes—how they twinkled! His dimples how merry!
His cheeks were like roses, his nose like a cherry!
His droll little mouth was drawn up like a bow,
And the beard on his chin was as white as the snow."

"He had a broad face and a little round belly,
That shook when he laughed like a bowlful of jelly.
He was chubby and plump …"

Even if you had never seen a picture of him, this description from the poem "A Visit from St. Nicholas" would enable most people to visualize St. Nicholas (Santa Claus).

Finish each drawing using the description provided.

1. Her hair looked like a frizzy dandelion gone to seed.

2. His eyes were set close together, giving him a sinister look.

3. As soon as I saw his huge grin and the laugh lines around his eyes, I knew I'd like James.

4. The manticore was a Greek mythological beast with a human face and ears, blue eyes, and three rows of sharp teeth in each jaw. It had the body and tail of a lion with a ball of poisoned spines on the end.

Name: _____ Date: _____

Paint a Word Picture

Would you be able to describe someone well enough for an artist to draw a picture of that person?

Use words and phrases to describe the features and physical characteristics of someone you know well, like a parent, friend, brother, sister, or other relative.

Male or female? _____   Age: _____

Height: _____   Weight: _____

Skin color: _____   Eye color: _____

Describe hair color and style: _____

_____

Describe the eyebrows: _____

Describe the nose: _____

Describe the mouth: _____

Describe the ears: _____

Does this person have pierced ears? One, or both? _____

Does he or she wear glasses? If so, describe them. _____

_____

What else is unique about the person's face? _____

_____

What type of clothing does this person usually wear? _____

_____

Describe any type of jewelry (rings, watch, necklace, earrings, etc.) this person usually wears.

_____

What would most people notice about this person if he or she were in a group of people about the same age? _____

_____

Describe the way this person walks. _____

Describe this person's voice. _____

Save this page to use with the next activity.

Name: _____ Date: _____

Options Available

A picture of a person could be a realistic photograph, a cartoon drawing, or an abstract painting. It could also be an action shot or a portrait. The picture could be done in pencil, charcoal, paint, or crayon.

Writing about a person can also be done in many different ways.

- You could write a physical description of someone.

- You could describe that person's character traits or focus on one particular trait, such as generosity or bravery.

- You could write about a particular memory you have of that person.

- You could write a humorous anecdote about someone.

- You could write a poem about him or her.

- You could make that person the main character in a play or short story.

- You could write a dialogue between yourself and that person.

- You could write him or her a letter.

- You could write a news article about something that person did.

1. Who will you write about? _____

2. Narrow your focus. What will be the main idea of your paragraph?

_____

_____

_____

3. Write about that person on your own paper. Use any style of writing (essay, poetry, short story, etc.).

4. When you finish, edit, revise, and proofread your work. If possible, draw a picture or add a photograph of that person.

5. The person you wrote about would probably enjoy reading what you wrote. If you'd like, share your writing with him or her.

Name: _____ Date: _____

What Does Freedom Mean to You?

You can describe an **abstract idea** by defining it and giving examples.

Some abstract ideas you could write about are:

love
charity
goodness
cooperation

respect
freedom
morality
consideration

bravery
honesty
patriotism
thoughtfulness

loyalty
kindness
friendship

1. Select one of the ideas listed or another abstract idea that is important to you. Write words and phrases to answer these questions.

    A. What does this idea mean to you?_____

    _____

    B. Why is it important? _____

    _____

    C. What makes a person honest or kind or brave or whatever characteristic you have chosen?

    _____

    _____

    D. What did you or someone else do that showed an example of this trait?

    _____

    _____

2. On your own paper, write about a character trait and what it means to you. Include your definition and an example of that trait.

3. Proofread, edit, and revise your work before rewriting.

Name: _____ Date: _____

Marcus Roared With Laughter

Lively verbs like *dashed, twirled, shivered,* and *frolicked* create more interesting and more precise details for the reader.

Lively verbs change dull sentences to interesting ones, and they provide a clearer picture of the action.

Dull: The child was afraid.   **More interesting:** The lost toddler shivered with fear.

Rewrite the sentences to make them more interesting by using action verbs and descriptive adjectives.

1. Tina was sad. _____

_____

2. Tim was happy. _____

_____

3. The snake made a noise. _____

_____

4. They were hungry. _____

_____

5. The cat and dog looked at each other. _____

_____

6. "I am leaving," he said. _____

_____

7. The thunder was loud. _____

_____

8. The flowers had a nice smell. _____

_____

9. The crowd was excited. _____

_____

10. He ate his spinach. _____

_____

Name: _____ Date: _____

The Horse Ran Fast

You can make your writing more interesting by adding adjectives, changing the word order in sentences, combining short sentences, and using *-ing* words.

Dull sentences: The horse ran fast. It ran down the mountain.

More interesting sentences: The silver horse bolted down the treacherous mountain trail.

The frightened horse thundered down the steep mountain trail like a streak of lightning.

Rewrite the sentences by changing the word order, using synonyms, combining sentences, adding adjectives, and/or using *-ing* words to make the sentences more interesting.

1. Sara felt good when she got a good grade on her test. _____

    _____

    _____

2. It was a cold day. The cold wind blew. Carlos was very cold.

    _____

    _____

    _____

3. The builder built a nice building. _____

    _____

    _____

4. It was a bad storm. Josh hid under the bed during the bad storm.

    _____

    _____

5. I like to eat turnips. Turnips are my favorite food. I could eat turnips every day.

    _____

    _____

Name: _____ Date: _____

Ready, Set, Action!

By using **action verbs** and **descriptive adjectives** in your writing, your readers will understand events clearly and feel like they are part of the scene.

1. On your own paper, write a paragraph to describe one of the scenes below. Use sensory words, action verbs, sentence variety, and descriptive adjectives.

   A sporting event: Describe a sporting event like a track meet, football game, stock-car race, or volleyball tournament. Write about the experience from the point of view of either a participant or a fan.

   Loop-de-loop: Describe a wild ride on a huge roller coaster from the point of view of someone on the ride.

   At the Olympics: Imagine being at the Olympics. Write about the experience from the point of view of either a participant or a spectator.

   Family get-together: Describe the people and events at a large family holiday get-together.

   A day at the zoo or circus: A zoo is filled with many sights, sounds, and smells. Describe a visit to a zoo or circus.

   The first day of school: The first day of class can be exciting and confusing, especially if you are attending a new school. Describe your first day at school this year.

   Moving time: Packing, moving, unpacking, and getting organized can be a lot of hard work. Describe a move you've made to a different house.

2. When you finish your first draft, edit, revise, and proofread your paragraph.

Name: _____ Date: _____

As Stubborn as a Mule

Similes are figures of speech that compare two unlike objects using the words *like* or *as.* Similes provide descriptive pictures of people, places, and things.

Examples: Her smile was **like** sunshine on a cloudy day.
The old prospector's skin was **as** brown and wrinkled **as** an old baked potato.

Finish the similes.

1. The moon shone as brightly as _____.

2. The fog enclosed us like _____.

3. Her hair looked like _____.

4. The cloud looked as fluffy as _____.

5. They were as _____ as _____.

6. She danced like a _____.

7. Her smile was as welcome as _____.

8. Grandpa's words made the boy feel as _____ as a

_____.

9. _____ was like a winter blizzard.

10. _____ was as _____ as a nest of hornets.

Write three similes of your own.

11. _____

_____

12. _____

_____

13. _____

_____

Name: _____ Date: _____

A Streak of Lightning

Metaphors are figures of speech that compare two unlike objects without using the words *like* or *as*.

1. Circle the two objects being compared in each sentence.

    A. The coach's mood was a thunderstorm after the game.

    B. The trip across the desert was a nightmare of light and heat.

    C. The mall was a zoo on Saturdays.

    D. The fog was a cat creeping silently through the night.

    E. The eagle was a streak of lightning across the sky.

Both items in a metaphor must be **nouns**. "Josh is sad" is not a metaphor because *sad* is an adjective, not a noun.

2. Complete the metaphors.

    A. The heat was _____
       (noun)

    B. The north wind is _____
       (noun)

    C. Her loneliness was _____
       (noun)

    D. The ferocious storm was _____
       (noun)

    E. The restless children were _____
       (noun)

    F. The creaking door was _____
       (noun)

    G. The mall was _____ at midnight.
       (noun)

3. Write a metaphor about a person. Circle both nouns.

    _____

    _____

4. Write a metaphor about an animal. Circle both nouns.

    _____

    _____

5. Write a metaphor about a weather-related event. Circle both nouns.

    _____

    _____

Name: _____ Date: _____

Opposites Attract

When writing comparison/contrast descriptions, you'll probably use many **antonyms**, which are words that have opposite meanings.

1. Write an antonym for each word. Use a dictionary or thesaurus if you need help.

    angry _____   adult _____

    bad _____   big _____

    cold _____   catch _____

    down _____   dull _____

    end _____   exit _____

    foolish _____   friendly _____

    good _____   high _____

    in _____   just _____

    kind _____   laugh _____

    love _____   major _____

    me _____   noon _____

    open _____   parent _____

    please _____   put _____

    quiet _____   sooner _____

    sunny _____   true _____

    ugly _____   up _____

    windy _____   winner _____

2. Write 10 words to describe an elephant.

    _____

    _____

    _____

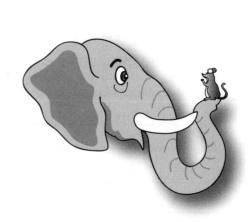

3. Write 10 words to describe a mouse.

    _____

    _____

    _____

Student Booster: Writing Description

Name: _____ Date: _____

Many types of writing include descriptions of the ways in which two people, objects, or ideas are alike and the ways in which they are different.

Creating a Venn Diagram can help you organize your ideas.

1. Write the names of two people on the lines.

2. In the portion where the two circles overlap, list similarities. For example: both people are male.

3. In the portion of each circle that does not overlap, list things that are different about each person, such as looks, personality, age, occupation, etc.

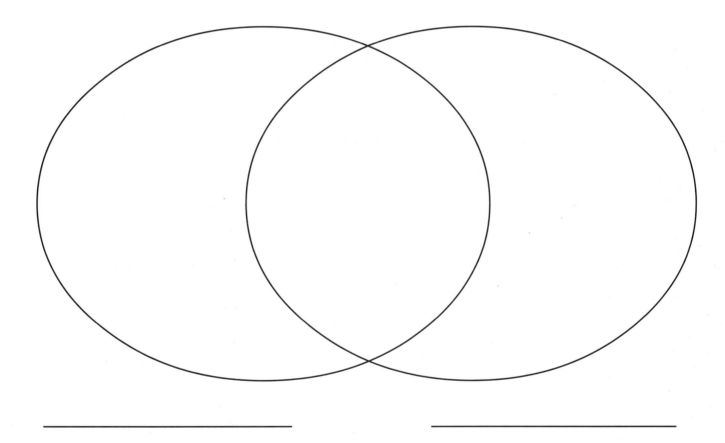

_____   _____

4. On your own paper, compare and contrast two people. Include at least one paragraph explaining the ways in which they are similar, and one explaining the ways in which they are different. Use descriptive words and lively verbs.

5. Proofread, edit, and revise your work.

6. If possible, add drawings or photographs of both people.

Name: _____ Date: _____

Like Walking on Eggs

Idioms are phrases that say one thing but actually mean something else. Idioms should be used sparingly when writing.

Circle the idiom in each sentence, and then write a brief explanation of what is actually meant.

1. When the Johnsons adopted their baby, the process involved a lot of red tape.

   _____

   _____

2. Last Saturday, it rained cats and dogs.

   _____

   _____

3. Our cousins in Ireland rolled out the red carpet when we went for a visit.

   _____

   _____

4. Cassie was a bundle of nerves on the first day at her new school.

   _____

   _____

5. Jay had butterflies in his stomach when he gave his speech.

   _____

   _____

6. Maria felt down in the dumps when her turtle ran away.

   _____

   _____

7. "It's a secret," whispered Todd, "so button your lip."

   _____

   _____

8. Mom blew her stack when she saw the mess in the kitchen.

   _____

   _____

Name: _____ Date: _____

Use the words in the clock to complete the activity. Write the correct term on the line after each statement.

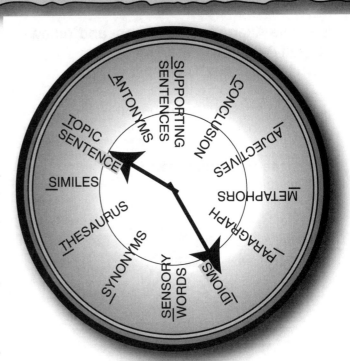

1. Figures of speech that compare two unlike objects using the words *like* or *as*

   _____

2. Phrases that say one thing, but actually mean something else

   _____

3. Words that describe nouns

   _____

4. Figures of speech that compare two unlike objects without using the words *like* or *as*

   _____

5. Words that mean the same, or nearly the same, thing _____

6. A sentence that sums up or restates the main idea of a paragraph _____

   _____

7. Words that describe senses _____

8. A book that lists synonyms _____

9. A group of sentences about a topic with a beginning, a middle, and a conclusion

   _____

10. Words that have opposite meanings _____

11. Sentences that provide descriptions, details, and examples

    _____

12. The first sentence of a paragraph _____

Answer Keys

A Purple Alien Wearing Green- and Yellow- Striped Pajamas (page 5)
1. large, shaggy, floppy
2. tiny, gray, long, thin
3. freckled, red, green, baseball
4. old, broken, sagging, moth

Finish the Pictures (page 17)
4. Manticore:

A Streak of Lightning (page 25)
A. mood — thunderstorm
B. trip — nightmare
C. mall — zoo
D. fog — cat
E. eagle — streak (of lightning)

Like Walking on Eggs (page 28)
1. red tape: paperwork; bureaucracy
2. rained cats and dogs: rained very hard
3. rolled out the red carpet: made someone feel very welcome/royal
4. bundle of nerves: worried or upset
5. butterflies in his stomach: nervous/scared
6. down in the dumps: depressed/sad
7. button your lip: keep silent
8. blew her stack: got very upset/angry

Time to Review (page 29)
1. similes
2. idioms
3. adjectives
4. metaphors
5. synonyms
6. conclusion
7. sensory words
8. thesaurus
9. paragraph
10. antonyms
11. supporting sentences
12. topic sentence